PEOPLE AT
THE CENTER OF

WORLD WAR I

By GAIL B. STEWART

BLACKBIRCH™
PRESS

THOMSON

GALE

San Diego • Detroit • New York • San Francisco • Cleveland
New Haven, Conn. • Waterville, Maine • London • Munich

THOMSON

GALE

LIBRARY OF CONGRESS CATALOGING-IN-PUBLICATION DATA

Stewart, Gail, 1949-
  World War I / by Gail B. Stewart.
    p. cm. — (People at the center of:)
Summary: Profiles people involved in World War I, including both political and military leaders on both sides of the conflict.
Includes bibliographical references and index.
  ISBN 1-56711-773-2 (hardback : alk. paper)
  1. World War, 1914-1918—Juvenile literature. [1. World War, 1914-1918—Biography.] I. Title: World War 1. II. Title: World War One.
III. Title. IV. Series.
  D522.7.S785 2004
  940.3'092'2—dc22
                                                    2003016805

Printed in United States
10 9 8 7 6 5 4 3 2 1

CONTENTS

PEOPLE AT THE CENTER OF

WORLD WAR I

It was a war on a scale that had never been imagined. People called it the "Great War," for an astonishing twenty-seven nations took part in the fighting, which went on for four long years. Historians estimate that between 1914 and 1918, approximately 65 million men were in uniform, and nearly 10 million of them died. In fact, France, Belgium, and other European nations—where most of the fighting took place—lost an entire generation of young men to the Great War.

Rumblings of war began years before the actual fighting started. Many European nations had begun to build up their stockpile of weapons. One of these was France, which had been defeated by Germany in a war in 1870 and stripped of two wealthy farming and mining provinces, Alsace and Lorraine, in eastern France. As a result of this loss, the French began to accumulate weapons to use in a future war against Germany. As France built up its arsenal, Germany followed.

Nations watched one another increase their production of weapons and, afraid that they would be unprepared in case of war, stepped up their own arms production. Besides building up their stockpiles of weapons, European nations began to protect themselves by forming agreements, or alliances, with other nations in case they were attacked. France, for example, signed alliances with both Britain and Russia. Those three nations were known as the Allies and promised to support one another against Germany. Germany and Austria-Hungary formed an alliance, too, and were known as the Central Powers.

The alliances were intended to prevent a war from beginning. Each side thought that presenting a strong, united team would make the other side less willing to start

After France was defeated by Germany in 1870, the French built up a weapons arsenal in case of future wars. Here, a French soldier fires an air torpedo during World War I.

trouble. The two alliances, however, only made the hostility between nations more severe. Europe in 1914 consisted of two heavily armed factions. The fear and anxiety, noted observers, were almost unbearable. One U.S. diplomat wrote that the tension in Europe was such that any small conflict could send the whole continent into war.

On June 28, 1914, that is exactly what happened. Archduke Francis Ferdinand, the heir to the throne of Austria-Hungary, was assassinated as he rode in a parade in Bosnia. The assassin was from the nearby kingdom of Serbia, which did not get along with Austria-Hungary. The government of Austria-Hungary declared war on Serbia. Russia, which had a large Serbian population, defended Serbia and prepared for war. When the Germans heard that Russia was going to fight, they began to mobilize their army to defend Austria-Hungary. Because of their alliance with Russia, France and Britain were pulled into the war, too.

Some nations tried to remain neutral, but it became almost impossible as the fighting started. Belgium, for example, had not signed an alliance with either of its neighbors, France or Germany. Germany did not respect Belgium's neutral status, however, and invaded the nation in August 1914 as it marched toward France. The United States tried to remain neutral, too. Woodrow Wilson, the president of the United States, had maintained a good relationship with both Germany and Britain and hoped that he would not have to take sides between those nations. As the war went on and German submarines attacked ships carrying American citizens, however, Wilson became angry. When warnings to Germany did not stop the attacks, the United States finally entered the war in 1917 as one of the Allies.

When Austria-Hungary declared war on Serbia, Russia prepared for war, setting off a chain of events that soon pulled in Germany, France, and Britain. Pictured here are Serbian soldiers in the trenches in 1915.

World War I was the first war in which airplanes were used.

World War I was remarkable, not only for the large number of armies that fought but for the types of weapons that were used. It was the first war in which airplanes and lighter-than-air zeppelins appeared. Tanks first made their appearance, as did chemical weapons. Clouds of chemicals, such as poisonous mustard gas, blinded and killed thousands of soldiers during this war. It was the first time submarines were effectively used in war, too.

The new weapons required a whole new sort of military strategy. No longer was it effective to send large numbers of troops rushing toward an enemy's position. There was no sense in preparing soldiers for hand-to-hand combat—either on foot or on horseback. In fact, with the huge new artillery weapons that were invented for this war, it was not even necessary to be able to see one's enemies to kill them. Thousands of soldiers—or civilians—could be killed with bombs dropped from high in the air or delivered by way of screaming artillery blasts from eighty miles away. Generals on both sides often continued to fight in the traditional ways and sent charges of men with rifles toward entrenched enemies with machine guns. The result was the senseless slaughter of millions of young soldiers.

World War I was also the first war in which civilians were involved by the millions. To the opposing army, they could be targets of bombs and artillery fire. To their own army, civilians were crucial for what they could produce. In the United States, for example, there was an increasing demand for the nation's farmers to

Much of the war was fought in France. By the end of the war, whole towns had been completely destroyed. Shown here are the ruins of Thiaucort, France, in 1918.

Thousands of civilians were killed by bombs dropped from the air during World War I. Here, girls stand over the grave of victims of an air raid.

produce more food and for factory workers to turn out more weapons, airplanes, and supplies—not only for American soldiers, but for the Allies. Civilians were also critically important in keeping the nation's morale high during the dark days of war.

When Germany and Austria-Hungary surrendered to the Allies on November 11, 1918, the world had become a very different place. People had seen the devastation that a modern war could cause. They saw the endless numbers of funerals for young men killed in battle and the countless numbers of soldiers who returned home wounded and scarred for life.

In January 1919, people throughout the world hoped that the Paris Peace Conference, a meeting to work out the terms of truce, could work out a plan for a lasting peace. They did not want to repeat the horrors of the past four years. As representatives tried to work out a viable peace plan, the people of the world celebrated the end of the most devastating war in history.

When the war finally ended in 1918, Allied soldiers celebrated with crowds of villagers all over France.

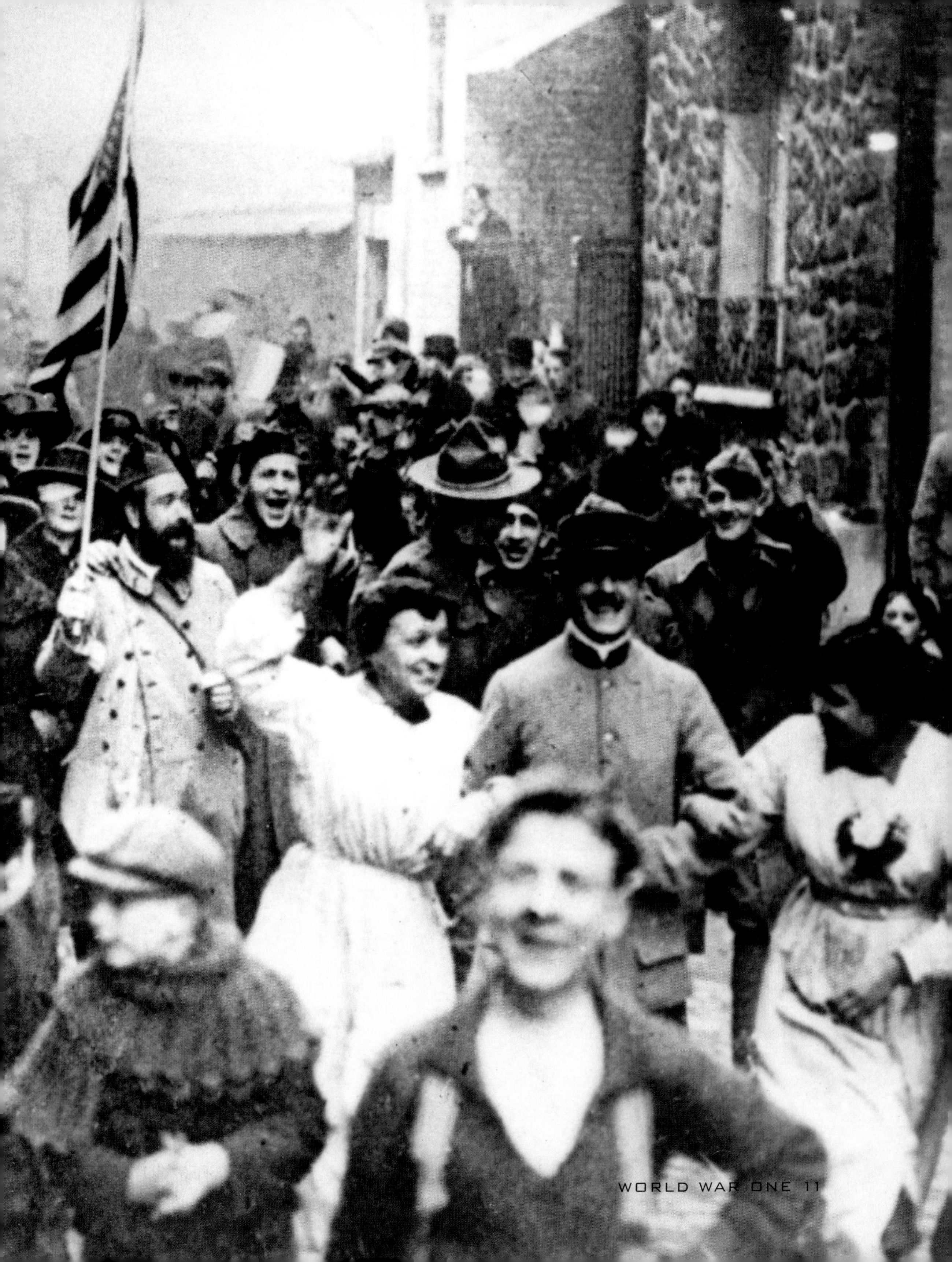

Born in Berlin, Germany, in 1859, Wilhelm was the oldest son of Frederick III and Princess Victoria, the daughter of Queen Victoria of England. Wilhelm's education was controlled by his grandfather, who was Kaiser (King) Wilhelm I. Wilhelm was trained in the military arts, and when his grandfather and father died within months of one another in 1888, the twenty-nine-year-old took the throne.

Above: Kaiser Wilhelm I was the first emperor of the German Empire. Opposite: Wilhelm II broke an alliance with Russia in 1890. This may have caused Germany's defeat in World War I.

Kaiser Wilhelm II believed it was very important for Germany to build up its military forces. In 1871, during the reign of his grandfather, Germany had crushed France in what came to be known as the "Lightning War" because of the speed of the victory. Since that time, France had worked to become stronger and to improve its military so that it would be prepared for a future war. Germany was doing the same, however. During Wilhelm's reign, he encouraged trade and manufacturing, especially the production of weapons and other war supplies, and Germany's economy prospered. He was especially eager to outdo France's ally, Britain, who had the world's mightiest navy. This rapid arms race between Germany and the Allies created tension throughout Europe in the months before war broke out.

Historians believe that Wilhelm's most critical error of the war actually occurred in 1890, long before the fighting began. It was then that he broke an important alliance with Russia. Russia became fearful of Germany and formed alliances with France and Britain. When the war began in 1914, Germany was forced to fight enemies on two fronts, which eventually led to Germany's defeat.

In November 1918, with Germany suffering food shortages and the nation close to defeat, Wilhelm was forced to give up his throne. He fled to the Netherlands, where he stayed until his death in 1941.

CZAR NICHOLAS II

THE LAST CZAR OF RUSSIA

Nicholas II was born in St. Petersburg, Russia, in 1868. His father, Alexander III, was the king, or czar. Although Nicholas received an excellent education as a boy, he was cut off from the real world, as were many children in royal families. As a result, he did not understand the poverty and dissatisfaction that millions of Russian people experienced every day.

When his father died in 1894, Nicholas took the throne as czar. The Russia he ruled was in severe economic trouble, and people were demanding reforms that would allow them the kinds of freedoms found in Western nations of Europe, such as freedom of speech and representation by lawmakers. Nicholas had been brought up to believe that the czar must have absolute power, however, and was reluctant to give in to the people's demands.

Early in the twentieth century, Nicholas began to fear Germany, especially because of Germany's rapid arms buildup. His fears increased when Germany formed an alliance, or agreement, with Austria-Hungary. Under this alliance, Austria-Hungary promised to support Germany in the event of an attack. For this reason, he entered into an alliance with France and Britain, so that if Russia were attacked, those nations would come to his aid. In 1914, when Austria-Hungary (an ally of Germany) declared war on tiny Serbia, with whom Nicholas also had an alliance, Russia was forced to enter the war, too.

Above: During the reign of Nicholas II, people all over Russia were starving. Opposite: Nicholas II was the last czar of Russia.

Russia was not prepared for war, and millions of Russian soldiers were killed for lack of guns and ammunition. There were no food or clothing supplies for the troops either, and many soldiers—cold and starving—simply left the battlefield in despair. Nicholas became distracted by more frequent civilian revolts, as well. Throughout the country, whole families were starving. Shortages of food and growing poverty made the millions of Russia's poor people angry at the czar.

In 1917, the government of Russia was taken over by a group of revolutionaries, and Nicholas and his family were forced to flee. There remains today great mystery about their fate. Some historians say that Nicholas and his family escaped during the revolt; however, most believe they were shot by the revolutionaries on July 18, 1918.

Hiram Maxim

Hiram Maxim was born in Sangerville, Maine, in 1840. Although he only attended school until the fourth grade, he was extremely gifted with mechanics. As a boy, he built models of machines he saw in his farming community. His first real invention was a mousetrap that was self-resetting.

In 1882, a friend told Maxim that if he wanted to make a fortune, he should invent a new sort of weapon, because it seemed that all of Europe was arming itself for war. Intrigued by the idea, Maxim focused his energy on the creation of a truly automatic gun. At the time, even the fastest marksman could fire a rifle only fifteen rounds in a minute. In his experiments, Maxim found that by using energy from the gun's recoil, the used shell would be extracted and a new one loaded into the barrel. A soldier could, with just a finger on the trigger, shoot more than four hundred rounds per minute.

Maxim offered his invention to both the U.S. Army and Navy, but neither thought it was practical. In 1891, he sold the machine gun—or "Maxim's Gun," as it was called—to the British. The British army took the machine guns to India and their African colonies and found them useful in putting down rebellions.

Above: Maxim's automatic gun could shoot more than four hundred rounds a minute. Opposite: When neither the U.S. Army nor Navy was interested in his machine gun, Hiram Maxim sold it to Britain.

Pleased by the reception he received in England, Maxim became a British citizen and was knighted by Queen Victoria for his contribution to the army.

By 1905, there were scores of armies and navies throughout the world who utilized the gun. When World War I began in 1914, both the German and Allied armies had machine gunners, but generals did not adapt their military strategies. In fact, thousands of soldiers were ordered to charge enemy positions with swords and rifles. Using a few machine guns, the entrenched army could easily kill the men as they charged. In time, the huge numbers of deaths from the machine guns finally forced a change in military strategy, but millions of soldiers died before commanding officers learned this lesson.

Maxim lived until 1916, long enough to see how his invention revolutionized warfare.

DAVID LLOYD GEORGE

LED GREAT BRITAIN DURING THE WAR

David Lloyd George was born on January 17, 1863, in Manchester, England. He became a lawyer as a young man and was elected as a member of the House of Commons at age twenty-seven, the youngest member of Parliament ever. As a member of the Liberal Party, he advocated a number of reforms that would help poor citizens.

In 1914, Germany invaded neutral Belgium on its way to attack France, with whom Britain had a treaty of alliance. Lloyd George was a pacifist and an outspoken critic of going to war with Germany. At first, he threatened to resign if Britain entered the war. After war was declared, however, he changed his position. He decided that since Britain was at war, the death toll of British soldiers would be far lower if the Allies won a quick victory. Lloyd George was appointed minister of munitions and worked to organize a rapid and steady flow of weapons and other supplies to the front. He was promoted to secretary of war and replaced Henry Asquith as prime minister in 1916.

One of the most important contributions Lloyd George made to the war was his solution to the growing problem with

Above: A German submarine surfaces. German submarines torpedoed hundreds of Allied supply ships. Opposite: When France and the United States disagreed about penalties for Germany after the war, David Lloyd George helped them reach a compromise.

Germany's submarines. So many British and Allied supply ships were being torpedoed that Britain was in danger of mass starvation. He devised the convoy system, a method of protecting every merchant ship with armed escorts. Although the system was more expensive, since it used more ships at one time, there were far fewer attacks by German submarines once it was used.

After the war, Lloyd George was an important part of the Paris Peace Conference. He was the voice of compromise between Premier Georges Clemenceau of France—who advocated harsh penalties for Germany—and President Woodrow Wilson of the United States—who advocated far more lenient measures. He resigned from Parliament in 1922 and never again sought public office. He died in January 1945.

ARCHDUKE FRANCIS FERDINAND

HIS ASSASSINATION TRIGGERED WORLD WAR I

Francis Ferdinand was born in Graz, Austria, in 1863. He was the son of Archduke Carl Ludwig, who was the brother of Austria's emperor, Franz Josef I. He finished his education at age twenty and began a military career. He was promoted rapidly because of his royal ties and expected to spend his adult life as a general in the Austrian army.

There were several untimely deaths in the family, however, and at age twenty-nine, Ferdinand was startled to find himself next in line for the empire's throne. He was irritated when family members urged him to marry a young woman of royal blood. He was far more interested in Sophie Chotek von Chotkva—not royalty, but a lady-in-waiting to a duchess. Even though it was shocking to high society in Austria and to his family, Ferdinand married Sophie in 1899. He was warned that his children would never be able to ascend to the throne, since Sophie was not of royal blood. Ferdinand was unconcerned.

It was not Ferdinand's life that was important to World War I, but his death. Relations between Austria-Hungary and the Balkans, states in southern Europe, were strained. Ferdinand

Above: Gavrilo Princip is seized after assassinating Archduke Ferdinand and his wife. Opposite: Franz Ferdinand, Archduke of Austria, is pictured here with his wife, Countess Choleck.

hoped that as heir to the throne, he could visit the Balkans and ease the tensions there. He and Sophie arranged to tour Bosnia in late June 1914. As the two rode though the capital city, Sarajevo, in a limousine, shots rang out. Within a few moments, Ferdinand and Sophie were dead.

The murderer was Gavrilo Princip, a young man from the nearby king-dom of Serbia, a region that had a history of quarrels with Austria. As the news of the assassination spread, it was clear that Austria would hold Serbia responsible for the murder. Serbia had allies, however. Russia, which had a large Serbian population, defended Serbia. If Russia was going to fight, then France and Britain would, too. That meant Germany would be drawn into the conflict. Within weeks of the murder of Ferdinand and his wife, Europe was at war.

The Great War lasted four years and involved 65 million soldiers from twenty-seven countries. In some European nations, it wiped out an entire generation of young men.

BARON MANFRED VON RICHTHOFEN

THE "RED BARON"

Manfred von Richthofen, or the "Red Baron," was born on May 2, 1892, to a well-to-do family of sheep farmers in Breslau, Germany. His father had been a military officer, and Manfred entered military school at age eleven. Although he was a bright student, he misbehaved in class and received poor grades. Even so, he was recruited by the German cavalry when he graduated because he was an exceptional horseback rider.

When war broke out in 1914, however, it soon became clear that a cavalry was now obsolete. With both armies in possession of rapid-firing machine guns capable of shooting more than four hundred rounds per minute, a charge on horseback would be suicidal for man and beast. So, von Richthofen transferred to the air service, where he learned to read aerial maps, drop bombs, and locate enemy troops from the air.

In September 1915, he began to fly missions over France and rapidly scored victory after victory. Even though he was highly skilled, von Richthofen was nervous that some of his fellow soldiers in the German army would mistake his plane for that of an Allied pilot, so he painted parts of the craft bright red. Because of his colorful plane and his ability to gun down other aircraft, von Richthofen became known as the "Red Baron." Later in the war, British pilots painted the noses of their planes red, to show that they were hunting for the Red Baron who was shooting their planes from the sky.

The Red Baron and his flying squadron shot down eighty enemy planes. Opposite: Baron Manfred von Richthofen was known as the greatest fighter pilot of World War I.

Von Richthofen accumulated several records for a war pilot. On April 29, 1917, he shot down four planes in one day. He also tallied an astonishing eighty victories during his career. He was killed on April 21, 1918, when his plane was shot down over France. His body was recovered by British and Australian troops, and he was buried with full military honors by armies who respected his skill—even though he fought for Germany.

Edith Cavell was born in Norwich, England, in 1865. The daughter of a minister, she had a strict upbringing that taught her to look for ways to help those in need. As a young woman, she worked as a governess in Belgium before she trained as a nurse in a London hospital. She returned to Belgium in 1907 and trained nurses in a Brussels clinic.

When war broke out in 1914, Cavell was in England visiting her mother. She quickly returned to Brussels to resume her work at the clinic. In the first part of the war, the clinic became a Red Cross hospital, which treated all wounded regardless of what army they fought for. When Brussels fell to the German army in 1915, however, the hospital was used strictly by the Germans for their own wounded men.

During this time, two British soldiers were separated from their unit behind enemy lines and found their way to Cavell's clinic. Aware that the men would be shot if they were discovered by the Germans, Cavell sheltered them for two weeks and then helped them escape to neutral Holland. Other Allied soldiers heard of Cavell and the clinic and came to her, too. The clinic became a sort of underground lifeline for nearly two hundred Allied soldiers, wounded and exhausted, to find refuge. After the soldiers were strong enough, Cavell and a few of the other nurses helped them escape to Holland.

Late in 1915, two of Cavell's coworkers were arrested, and she herself was put in prison after the German authorities discovered what was going on virtually under their noses. Cavell was questioned and gave a full confession. Afterward, she was sentenced to death by firing squad on October 12, 1915. Stories circulated after her death that several German soldiers had refused to take part in the firing squad and had also been executed.

Cavell's death had some interesting aftereffects. Recruitment totals in England and France doubled in the eight weeks after her execution. In addition, the stories in the press about her heroic deeds fueled the rumors of German atrocities and made citizens of Allied countries much more supportive of the war. At the war's end, Cavell was commemorated for her bravery by a statue in London's Trafalgar Square.

Red Cross nurse Edith Cavell helped almost two hundred wounded Allied soldiers escape into neutral Holland. When the Germans found out, she was put to death by a firing squad.

FERDINAND VON ZEPPELIN

Ferdinand von Zeppelin was born in Germany on July 8, 1838. As a young man, he joined the German army and was part of a group who went to the United States during the Civil War to observe the Union army. After the war ended in 1865, he took part in an expedition in Minnesota that was investigating the source of the Mississippi River. While on that expedition, Zeppelin had his first hot air balloon ride and enjoyed it immensely.

Zeppelins could carry more than a ton of bombs. Because they were quiet, the Germans used them in air raids over England and France.

At age fifty-three, Zeppelin retired from the army and devoted his time to studying what had become his first love—flying. He was interested in the design of a huge, cigar-shaped airship that could be filled with hydrogen gas and used in warfare. His airship would be an improvement over a regular hot air balloon, however, because it would have a steel frame that made it stronger. It would also be able to fly much higher than ordinary hot air balloons because of the enormous size of the ship's hydrogen gas tanks.

Zeppelin invested his own money in a factory for the airships, which he called zeppelins. By 1898, he and his staff of thirty workers had assembled the first of his airships. It weighed twelve tons and its frame was covered with fabric. He sold seven to the German army. Commanders were thrilled with the design and planned to use the airships for reconnaissance missions to observe the position and movement of the enemy's forces.

Zeppelin insisted the airships could do far more than carry observers, however. He equipped them with machine guns and the capacity for more than a ton of bombs. The German army saw more possibilities and began to use zeppelins for air raids against both England and France. Because they were quiet, the zeppelins could glide over a large city such as London and begin to drop bombs before anyone knew they were there. Their tremendous size and stealth made the zeppelins a powerful

Ferdinand von Zeppelin got his idea for an airship after flying in a hot air balloon.

psychological weapon. The British civilians were especially frightened of the airship, and morale suffered as a result of what became known as "zeppelin-itis," the fear of night attacks by the airships.

Zeppelin continued to build his airships until 1917, when cities began to use powerful searchlights and special artillery guns to shoot at the airships before they could do much damage. By the end of the war, they were used primarily for transporting machines and supplies. Zeppelin died in Germany in 1917, before the war ended.

Margaretha Zelle was born in Zeewarden, Holland, on August 7, 1876. In a region where most people are blue-eyed and blond, Zelle was olive-skinned, with dark hair and almost black eyes. As a girl she was popular and smart, with an amazing talent for learning languages quickly. At eighteen she married Rudolph Macleod, a military man, and moved with him to Indonesia. The marriage was a stormy one, however. Her husband was a heavy drinker and often abused her. Eventually, she divorced him and moved to Paris to find work.

In 1905, she became an exotic dancer and took the stage name Mata Hari, which is the Malay word for "sun." She dressed in ornate, jeweled tops and silky skirts and slacks and often wore a headdress or turban to make herself look more exotic. She began to give private nude performances of her dances in exchange for money and soon had a loyal following among the wealthiest men in Paris. In 1914, one of her clients, who belonged to the German Secret Service, recruited her to gather information from some of the French diplomats she was involved with. For months she transmitted information about troop movements and other secrets to Germany, using her code name "H-21."

Above: Mata Hari was imprisoned in St. Lazare Prison (pictured) in France for her espionage activities. Opposite: Magaretha Zelle, who used the stage name Mata Hari, was an exotic dancer who spied for both sides during the war.

In 1916, French intelligence agents suspected her of espionage, and when they tried to deport her, Mata Hari offered to spy for the Allies instead of the Germans. Allied agents soon discovered, however, that while she claimed to be spying for them, she was continuing to take money from Germany. In February 1917, she was arrested for treason and espionage by French intelligence officers and was sentenced to death. On October 15, despite protests from many of her former clients, she was executed by a firing squad.

WOODROW WILSON

Thomas Woodrow Wilson was born in Staunton, Virginia, on December 28, 1856. His father, a Presbyterian minister, told young Wilson stories of firsthand experiences in the Civil War. After he graduated from the College of New Jersey (which later became Princeton University), Wilson went to law school and later returned to Princeton as its president. He was elected governor of New Jersey in 1911 and in 1912 he became president of the United States.

When World War I began, Wilson was emphatic about keeping the United States out of war. He felt strongly that if both sides of the conflict could sit down and discuss the problems, the war could end—and he volunteered to mediate the discussions himself. There was no mediation, however, and Wilson continued to insist that the United States remain neutral.

On May 7, 1915, a German submarine torpedoed and sank the British passenger ship *Lusitania*, killing 128 Americans. Some Americans wanted to enter the war afterward, but Wilson still believed the United States could remain neutral. He negotiated with the German government and received assurances that no more neutral or passenger ships would be attacked. In February 1917, however, Germany began unrestricted torpedoing of all ships, including those from the United States. Wilson asked Congress for a declaration of war, and Congress agreed.

Once the United States was at war, Wilson did a great deal to mobilize the nation. He urged farmers to increase the amount of crops they grew and encouraged factories to add extra shifts and step up production so that the troops and America's allies were well provided for. On January 8, 1917, Wilson delivered an important speech to Congress. In the speech, he outlined fourteen points that he felt should be used in a settlement when the war was over. One of the most important points, he believed, was the establishment of a league of nations, a forum where world leaders could come together and resolve conflicts before they erupted into war.

When the war ended, Wilson went to France to participate in the Paris Peace Conference. The final treaty was approved by other nations, but Wilson was saddened that the U.S. Congress refused to accept the League of Nations. Members of Congress feared that U.S. interests might be compromised if such an organization existed, or that it might lead to further entangles with other nations. Wilson traveled around the country to rally support for the league but suffered a stroke. He died in 1924.

In 1917 Woodrow Wilson finally realized he had to ask Congress for a declaration of war.

SIR ERNEST SWINTON

DEVELOPED THE TANK

Ernest Swinton, a British citizen, was born in Bangalore, India, in 1864. He served in the British army as a young man, and was commissioned into the Corps of Royal Engineers in 1888. He served in the Second Boer War in Africa between 1899 and 1902. When World War I began, the British War Department sent him to the war's front in France. His job was to write detailed reports about the battles he witnessed.

One of the observations that most upset him was the ease in which British infantry soldiers were being killed by German machine gunners. As the gunners hid in the trenches they had dug, they wiped out whole units of men—thousands at a time, in some cases. During his time at the front, Swinton also happened to notice a tractor that used a caterpillar tread mechanism to transport heavy guns and other machinery on the battlefield. That gave him an idea.

Swinton designed a new weapon, which he called a "landship." Putting thick armored plates on a farm tractor allowed the vehicle to be driven straight at the machine gunners in their trenches. Because it would have the caterpillar treads, it would be able to plow through mud, artillery craters, and even the barbed wire set up around the machine gunners' trenches.

Few of Swinton's superiors in the army took his idea seriously; however, the lord of the navy, Winston Churchill, was interested. The navy needed large armored vehicles that could cross difficult terrain on the coasts of Belgium, and the landships might be the answer. In the months that followed, designers modified the original plan and created guns for the top of the vehicle, which became known as a tank because of its shape. Swinton's tanks made their first appearance in the Battle of the Somme, on September 16, 1916. The German troops panicked at the sight of forty-nine tanks rumbling toward their line, and the British were able to move forward and seize new territory as the Germans fled.

Swinton was made an honorary major general after the war because of his contribution to the Allied victory. He taught military history at Oxford University in England and died in 1951.

While working as a war correspondent on the front lines in France, Ernest Swinton saw British infantry soldiers being killed by German machine gunners. His landship design eventually developed into armored tanks that could withstand the machine gun.

John "Black Jack" Pershing

Commanded American forces in World War I

John Pershing was born in 1860, in Laclede, Missouri. He studied to be a teacher but changed his mind and entered the U.S. Military Academy at West Point when he was twenty-two. He graduated with honors in 1886 and began his military career in wars against the Apache Indians. He served in the Spanish-American War in 1898, in the Philippines, and in Mexico, where skirmishes broke out in 1914. It was in the Mexican campaign that he earned his nickname, "Black Jack," by commanding a troop that consisted solely of African Americans.

Above: "Black Jack" Pershing arrived in France as the commander of the American Expeditionary Force in 1917. Opposite: General Pershing's open field combat strategy helped to win the war.

Pershing was a tireless worker who stayed up very late each night to plan for the following day. Those who knew him best understood that he worked hard so that he would not have time to think about the fire in his family's army barracks that had killed his wife and three daughters in 1912. He confided to one friend that he never had anything to smile about after that day.

When the United States entered World War I in 1917, Pershing was sent to France as the commander of the 2.5-million-man American Expeditionary Force, or AEF. The French and British generals wanted to use the large American army to fill in gaps in their existing armies, which had been badly depleted in the fighting. Pershing insisted, however, that the AEF remain intact and fight independently. Although the Allied military leaders were opposed to the idea, they finally agreed.

Pershing knew that if the Allies were to win the war, they had to change the way they were fighting. Almost since the war began, the Allies had been fighting in a virtual stalemate of trench warfare against the German army. Pershing had trained his American troops in open field combat, not trench warfare. By using air support, tanks, and well-timed raids, they were able to push back the German line.

When World War I ended, Pershing remained in France to oversee the demobilization of the troops returning to the United States. He served as chief of staff for the U.S. Army until he retired in 1924. He died in 1948 and was buried in Arlington National Cemetery.

EDDIE RICKENBACKER

AMERICAN FIGHTER ACE

Eddie Rickenbacker was born in 1890, in Columbus, Ohio. His father died when Eddie was twelve, and he quit school to take odd jobs to support his family. As a young boy, he was fascinated with machines and automobiles, and at age nineteen he became a racer for the Firestone company. By 1915, he had become one of the most talented race car drivers in the United States.

When the United States entered the war in 1917, Rickenbacker enlisted in the army. He was assigned to be the personal driver of the commander of the U.S. forces, General John Pershing. He soon realized, however, that he would much rather become part of the newly formed Air Corps. Even though Rickenbacker had never flown a plane, he was confident that he could do well as a fighter pilot.

Rickenbacker was unlike other young men who became war pilots because he came from a poor family. Most pilots in the early days of airplanes were from wealthy families and could afford to spend time and money learning to fly.

Above: Before the war, Eddie Rickenbacker was one of the best race-car drivers in the United States. Opposite: Rickenbacker had twenty-six victories against the Germans.

Early in 1918, Rickenbacker completed his training and was assigned to the 94th Aero pursuit squadron in France. It was the first all-American air unit to see combat. Rickenbacker was a skilled pilot, and he soon earned the respect of everyone in his squad. He won France's Croie de la Guerre (War Cross) for shooting down five German airplanes. In all, Rickenbacker had twenty-six victories in the air against the Germans—his last on the day before the war ended. He was given the Congressional Medal of Honor for his outstanding record.

After the war, he started the Rickenbacker Motor Company, which produced the first American car with four-wheel brakes. He also worked for the Cadillac division of General Motors and later transferred to the aviation division of the company. He wrote his memoir, *Fighting the Flying Circus*, and died in Switzerland in 1973.

George Creel was born in Lafayette County, Missouri, in 1876. He was eager to become a newspaper reporter, and after he graduated from high school, he landed a job on the *Kansas City World*. From there, he worked on a number of other newspapers, which included the *New York Journal*, the *Denver Post*, and later his own newspaper, called the *Independent*. Creel was a strong supporter of U.S. president Woodrow Wilson and in 1916 worked to help reelect Wilson.

THIRD
UNITED STATES OFFICIAL WAR PICTURE
UNDER FOUR FLAGS
PRESENTED BY DIVISION OF FILMS
COMMITTEE ON PUBLIC INFORMATION
GEORGE CREEL, CHAIRMAN

Above: Pictured here is a poster for a movie supporting the war called Under Four Flags.
Opposite: During the war, George Creel was head of the Committee on Public Information. He helped to inspire patriotism.

When the United States entered the war in 1917, Wilson knew that the war effort required that Americans be enthusiastic and supportive. They would be asked to make a number of sacrifices for the war, and those challenges would be met more easily if they had a sense of patriotism and enthusiasm. To accomplish this, Wilson appointed Creel to head the Committee on Public Information, or CPI.

Creel and the CPI used every possible tool to inspire feelings of patriotism in Americans. They encouraged Hollywood to make films with war themes in hopes that such films would depict military heroes and make people proud to be Americans. As the CPI worked to put American soldiers in a positive light, Creel and his workers depicted Germans as evil. Exaggerated or made-up stories of German war crimes and atrocities against civilians made the American public dislike Germans even more and reminded people why the United States was fighting. One of Creel's most effective programs in the CPI was the "Four Minute Men." These were seventy-five thousand men who traveled around the country and gave four-minute speeches about the war. Often they stood up in restaurants or spoke in movie theaters right before or after the main feature. They were interesting speakers and were very popular with the public.

After the war, Creel wrote his memoir, *How We Advertised America*. He sought the Democratic nomination for governor of California in 1934, but was unsuccessful. He died in 1953 at age seventy-six.

GEORGES CLEMENCEAU

THE "TIGER OF FRANCE"

Georges Clemenceau was born on September 28, 1841, in Vendee, France. His father was an admirer of revolutionary politics, and Clemenceau grew up with a respect for people who fought for freedom and social justice. He wanted to become a doctor and, after he graduated from a Paris medical school, lived in New York for four years. When he returned to France, he became involved in politics for the first time. He first served in the National Assembly, the legislative body of France, and then as commissioner of foreign affairs.

In 1911, Clemenceau became fearful that Germany was arming itself for war and called for the French war department to do likewise. When France declared war on Germany in 1914, Clemenceau was installed as minister of war and government. He rallied support for the war effort among the French people, who were discouraged by

Above: When the Treaty of Versailles was drafted, Georges Clemenceau was adamant that Germany should be forced to pay for all the damages France had suffered. Opposite: Clemenceau, the "Tiger of France," was determined to defeat Germany.

the millions of young men being killed. He was known by his nickname of the "Tiger of France" because of his fierce determination to defeat Germany.

Clemenceau's most difficult fight occurred after the war, however. He presided over the Paris Peace Conference, where world leaders met to discuss the terms of Germany's surrender. Because so much of the war was fought in France and so many homes and businesses were destroyed, he was determined that Germany be forced to pay for the damage. He wanted to make certain that Germany would never be a threat to France or any other nation in Europe in the future. Although he compromised on a few points, the terms hammered out in the resulting document, called the Treaty of Versailles, treated Germany harshly. Massive war debts crippled Germany's economy, and its military was dismantled.

Clemenceau retired from politics in 1920 and died in 1929.

⊚ CHRONOLOGY

1871	Germany defeats France in the "Lightning War" and takes two of France's most valuable provinces, Alsace and Lorraine.
1891	Hiram Maxim develops the machine gun.
1898	Ferdinand von Zeppelin completes his first airship and sells it to the German army.
June 28, 1914	Archduke Francis Ferdinand and his wife Sophie are assassinated in Sarajevo, Bosnia.
July 28, 1914	Austria-Hungary declares war on Serbia.
August 4, 1914	Germany declares war on France, invades neutral Belgium.
May 7, 1915	German submarine sinks the passenger liner *Lusitania*.
October 12, 1915	Edith Cavell is executed by German army for helping Allied soldiers escape to Holland.
September 1916	First tanks used by Britain at the Battle of the Somme in France.
April 6, 1917	The United States declares war on Germany.
July 1917	Czar Nicholas II is forced to step down in Russia because of rioting and dissent.
April 21, 1918	The Red Baron is shot down.
November 11, 1918	Germany signs the armistice that officially ends World War I.

Tanks, chemical weapons, airplanes, and zeppelins were used for the first time in the "Great War" and contributed to the Allied victory. Shown here is a British tank in 1917.

FOR FURTHER INFORMATION

BOOKS

Craig Blohm, *Leaders and Generals: World War I*. San Diego: Lucent Books, 2002.

Michael L. Cooper, *Hell Fighters: African American Soldiers in World War I*. New York: Lodestar Books, 1997.

Stewart Ross, *War in the Trenches*. New York: Bookwright Press, 1991.

Gail B. Stewart, *Weapons of War: World War I*. San Diego: Lucent Books, 2002.

WEBSITES

Encyclopedia of the First World War
www.spartacus.schoolnet.co.uk
Very thorough treatment of a variety of categories, from weapons to generals, from artists of World War I to the war in the air. Great illustrations.

Hellfire Corner: The Great War-1914–1918
www.fylde.demon.co.uk
Excellent collection of first-person accounts of various battles during the war.

World War I: Trenches on the Web
www.worldwar1.com
Exciting site, with details about battles, life in the trenches, and the political scene during the war.

Gail B. Stewart received her undergraduate degree from Gustavus Adolphus College in St. Peter, Minnesota. She did her graduate work in English, linguistics, and curriculum study at the College of St. Thomas and the University of Minnesota. She taught English and reading for more than ten years. She has written more than ninety books for young people, including a series for Lucent Books called The Other America. She has written many books on historical topics such as World War I and the Warsaw ghetto. Stewart and her husband live in Minneapolis with their three sons, Ted, Elliot, and Flynn; two dogs; and a cat. When she is not writing she enjoys reading, walking, and watching her sons play soccer.